Double Stop Etudes for the Violin, book one

by Cassia Harvey
and Myanna Harvey

CHP406

©2021 by C. Harvey Publications All Rights Reserved.

www.charveypublications.com - print books
www.learnstrings.com - PDF downloadable books
www.harveystringarrangements.com - chamber music

Table of Contents

Section	Page
How to Practice This Book	a
Part One - D Major	2
Sixths	2
Thirds	6
Octaves	10
Fourths	13
Fifths	15
Slurs	16
Part Two - G Major	17
Sixths	17
Thirds	19
Octaves	23
Fourths	24
Fifths	25
Slurs	26
Part Three - C Major	27
Sixths	27
Thirds	29
Octaves	33
Fourths	34
Fifths	35
Slurs	36
Part Four - F Major	37
Sixths	37
Thirds	39
Octaves	42
Fourths	43
Fifths	44
Slurs	45
Part Five - B-flat Major	46
Sixths	46
Thirds	48
Octaves	51
Fourths	52
Fifths	53
Slurs	54
Part Six - Double Stop Scales in Other Keys	55

How to Practice this Book

- Each exercise goes with the etude that directly follows it.
- **Practice all of the exercises and etudes slowly at first.**
- Focus on learning the finger spacing patterns in each exercise so that you can use them in the etude.
- Add these exercises to your practice routine after finger exercises and scales and before repertoire.

Playing in Tune

- If a double stop is not in tune, play the notes separately and then together to correct the intonation.
- Playing double stops with too much force can make it difficult to hear the intonation. Keep the dynamic level to *mp* or *mf.*
- Continuously check notes with open strings when available (3rd finger with the open string below it and 4th finger with the open string above it.)

Getting Good Tone on Double Stops

- Make sure your bow is evenly balanced across the two strings.
- Play these studies *mp* or *mf* to help you hear if the bow is balanced. Playing with too much force in the bow can make it harder to hear whether the bow is balanced.
- Keep the bow moving; don't get stuck. Use enough bow to allow the strings to ring.
- Press both fingers into the strings completely and evenly. If one finger is not stopping the string, the note will sound flat and may squeak.
- Focus on intonation. Double stops that are in tune will ring and give you good tone!

Part One: D Major

Double Stop Etudes for the Violin, Book One

Exercises by Cassia Harvey
Etudes by Myanna Harvey

D Major Scale in Sixths (Low)

String Crossing in the D Major Scale

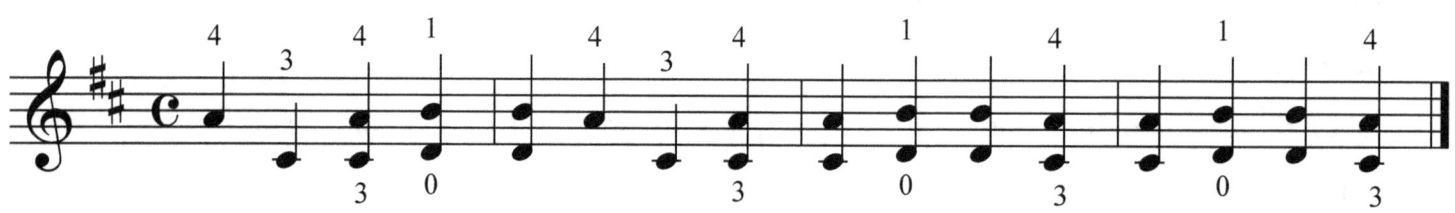

Finger Pattern Changes in the D Major Scale

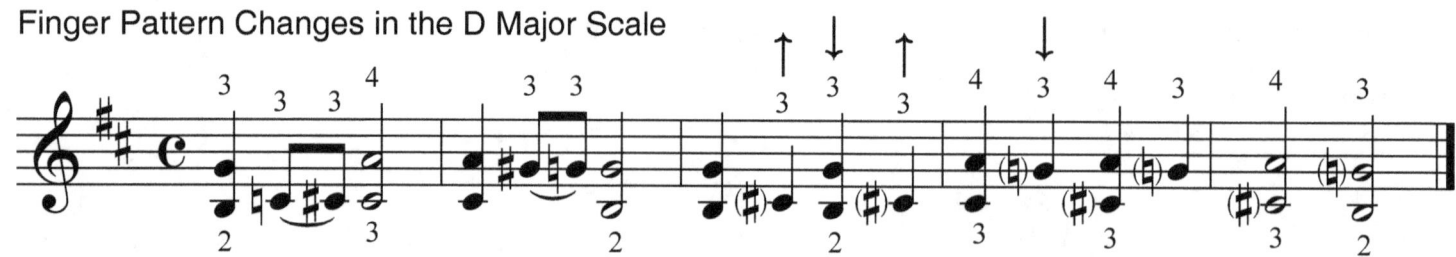

©2021 C. Harvey Publications All Rights Reserved.

Double Stop Etudes for the Violin, Book One

Sixths Etude No. 1

Sixths Etude No. 2

©2021 C. Harvey Publications All Rights Reserved.

Double Stop Etudes for the Violin, Book One

D Major Fragment in Sixths (High)

String Crossing in the D Major Fragment

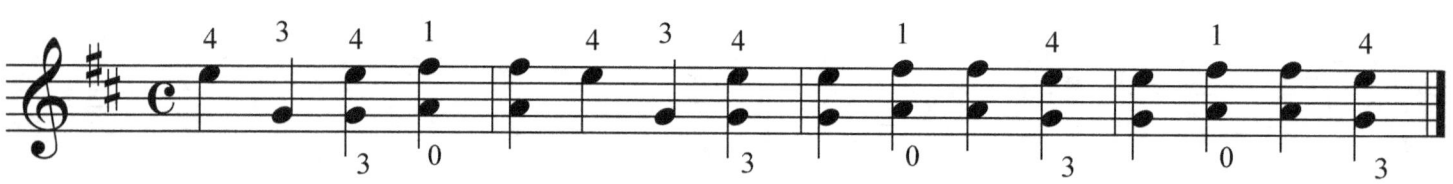

Finger Pattern Changes in the D Major Fragment

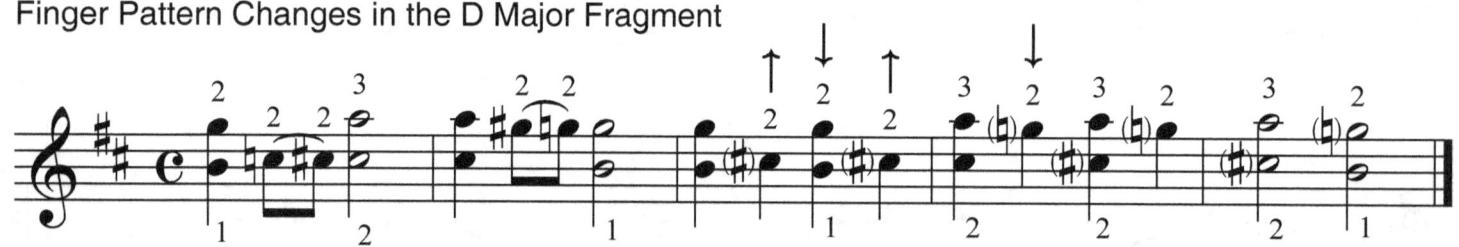

©2021 C. Harvey Publications All Rights Reserved.

Double Stop Etudes for the Violin, Book One

Sixths Etude No. 3

Sixths Etude No. 4

©2021 C. Harvey Publications All Rights Reserved.

D Major Exercise in Thirds (Low)

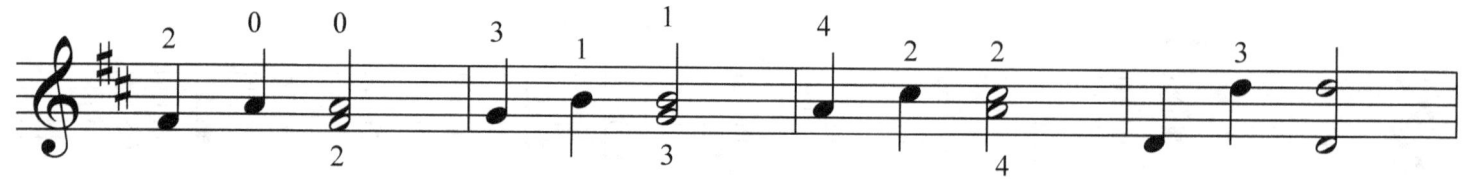

D Major Scale in Thirds (Low)

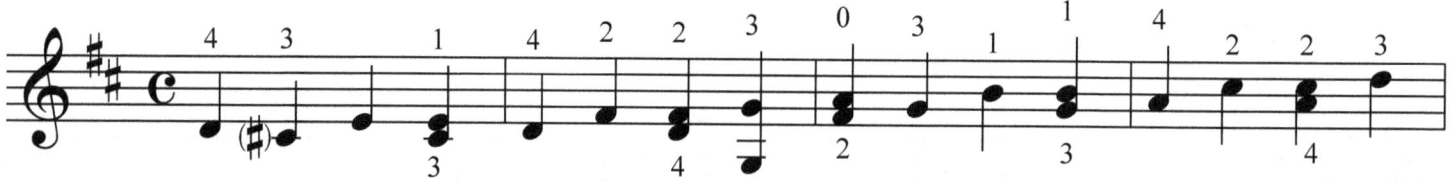
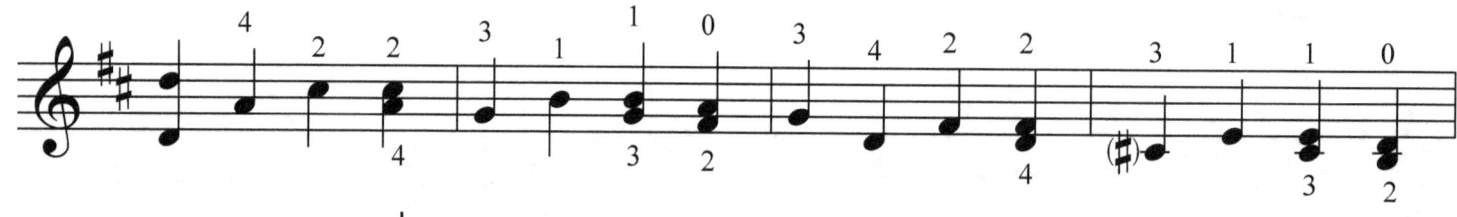
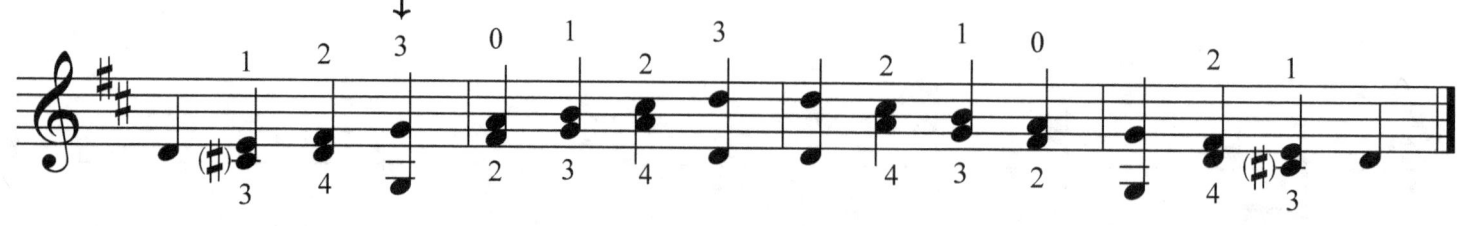

©2021 C. Harvey Publications All Rights Reserved.

Double Stop Etudes for the Violin, Book One

Thirds Etude No. 1

Thirds Etude No. 2

©2021 C. Harvey Publications All Rights Reserved.

Double Stop Etudes for the Violin, Book One

D Major Fragment in Thirds (High)

Thirds Etude No. 3

©2021 C. Harvey Publications All Rights Reserved.

Double Stop Etudes for the Violin, Book One

Thirds Etude No. 4

Thirds Etude No. 5

©2021 C. Harvey Publications All Rights Reserved.

Double Stop Etudes for the Violin, Book One

D Major Scale with Octaves

Octaves Etude No. 1

©2021 C. Harvey Publications All Rights Reserved.

Double Stop Etudes for the Violin, Book One

D Major Scale Combination No. 1

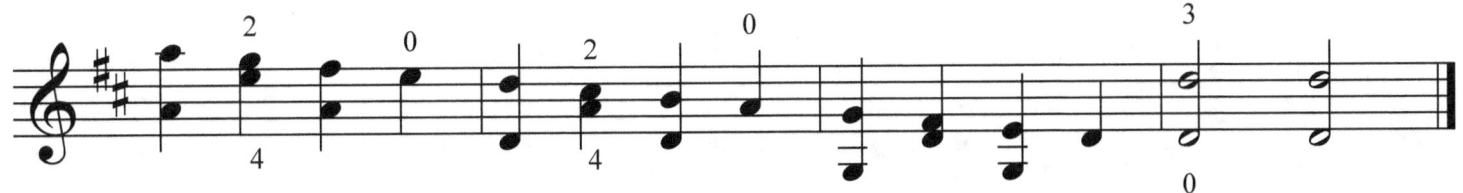

D Major Scale Combination No. 2

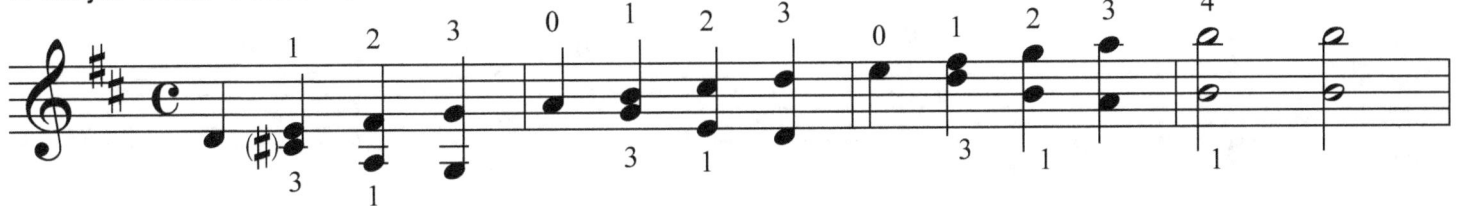
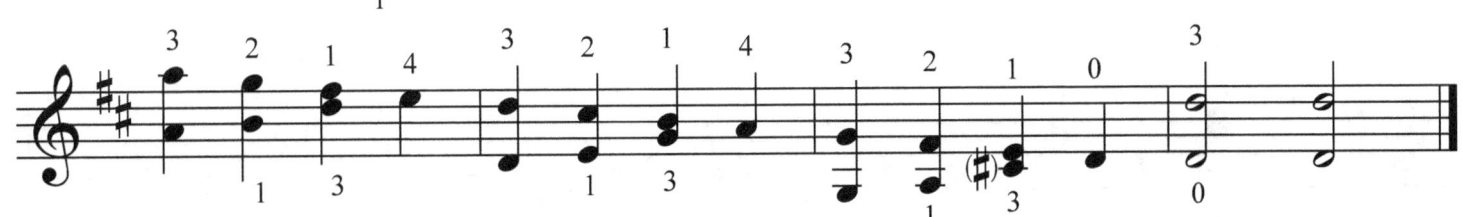

Combination Etude No. 1

©2021 C. Harvey Publications All Rights Reserved.

Double Stop Etudes for the Violin, Book One

D Major Scale Combination No. 3

D Major Scale Combination No. 4

Combination Etude No. 2

©2021 C. Harvey Publications All Rights Reserved.

Double Stop Etudes for the Violin, Book One
13

D Major Exercise in Fourths

D Major Scale in Fourths

©2021 C. Harvey Publications All Rights Reserved.

Double Stop Etudes for the Violin, Book One

Fourths Etude No. 1

Fourths Etude No. 2

Double Stop Etudes for the Violin, Book One

D Major Exercise in Fifths

Fifths Etude No. 1

©2021 C. Harvey Publications All Rights Reserved.

Double Stop Etudes for the Violin, Book One

D Major: Changing Notes While Holding Notes

Slur Etude No. 1

©2021 C. Harvey Publications All Rights Reserved.

Double Stop Etudes for the Violin, Book One

Part Two: G Major

G Major Exercise in Sixths

Sixths Etude No. 5

©2021 C. Harvey Publications All Rights Reserved.

Double Stop Etudes for the Violin, Book One

Crossing Strings in Double Stops

Low and High Second Finger

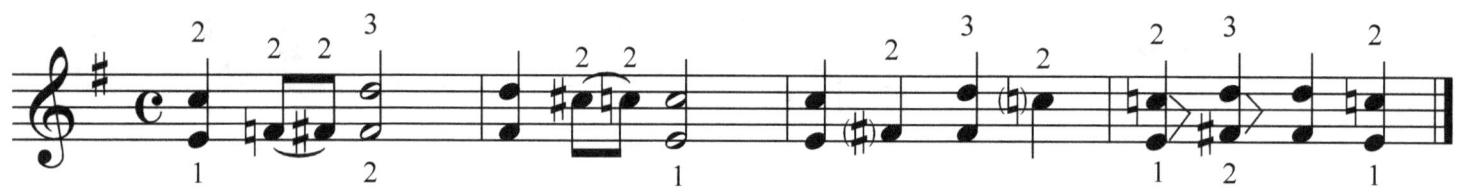

Sixths Etude No. 6

Double Stop Etudes for the Violin, Book One

G Major Scale in Thirds

Low and High Second Finger

Thirds Etude No. 6

Thirds Etude No. 7

Double Stop Etudes for the Violin, Book One

G Major Scale in Thirds and Octaves

Combination Etude No. 3

©2021 C. Harvey Publications All Rights Reserved.

22

Double Stop Etudes for the Violin, Book One

G Major Sixths and Thirds

Combination Etude No. 4

©2021 C. Harvey Publications All Rights Reserved.

Double Stop Etudes for the Violin, Book One

G Major Octave Exercise

Combination Etude No. 5

©2021 C. Harvey Publications All Rights Reserved.

24

Double Stop Etudes for the Violin, Book One

G Major Exercise in Fourths

Fourths Etude No. 3

©2021 C. Harvey Publications All Rights Reserved.

Double Stop Etudes for the Violin, Book One

G Major Exercise in Fifths

Fifths Etude No. 2

Double Stop Etudes for the Violin, Book One

G Major: Changing Notes While Holding Notes

Slur Etude No. 2

©2021 C. Harvey Publications All Rights Reserved.

Part Three: C Major

Learning Sixths in C Major

Sixths Etude No. 7

Double Stop Etudes for the Violin, Book One

C Major Scale in Sixths

Sixths Etude No. 8

Double Stop Etudes for the Violin, Book One

Learning Thirds in C Major

Thirds Etude No. 8

©2021 C. Harvey Publications All Rights Reserved.

C Major Scale Exercise in Thirds

Double Stop Etudes for the Violin, Book One

Thirds Etude No. 9

Thirds Etude No. 10

Double Stop Etudes for the Violin, Book One

C Major Exercise in Thirds and Sixths

Combination Etude No. 6

©2021 C. Harvey Publications All Rights Reserved.

Double Stop Etudes for the Violin, Book One

C Major Exercise High and Low First Finger

C Major Exercise in Octaves

Combination Etude No. 7

©2021 C. Harvey Publications All Rights Reserved.

34

Double Stop Etudes for the Violin, Book One

C Major Exercise in Fourths

Fourths Etude No. 4

©2021 C. Harvey Publications All Rights Reserved.

Double Stop Etudes for the Violin, Book One

C Major Exercise in Fifths

Fifths Etude No. 3

©2021 C. Harvey Publications All Rights Reserved.

C Major: Changing Notes While Holding Notes

Slurs Etude No. 3

Part Four: F Major

Learning Sixths in F Major

Sixths Etude No. 9

Double Stop Etudes for the Violin, Book One

F Major Scale in Sixths

Sixths Etude No. 10

©2021 C. Harvey Publications All Rights Reserved.

Double Stop Etudes for the Violin, Book One

Learning Thirds in F Major

Thirds Etude No. 11

Double Stop Etudes for the Violin, Book One

F Major Scale in Thirds

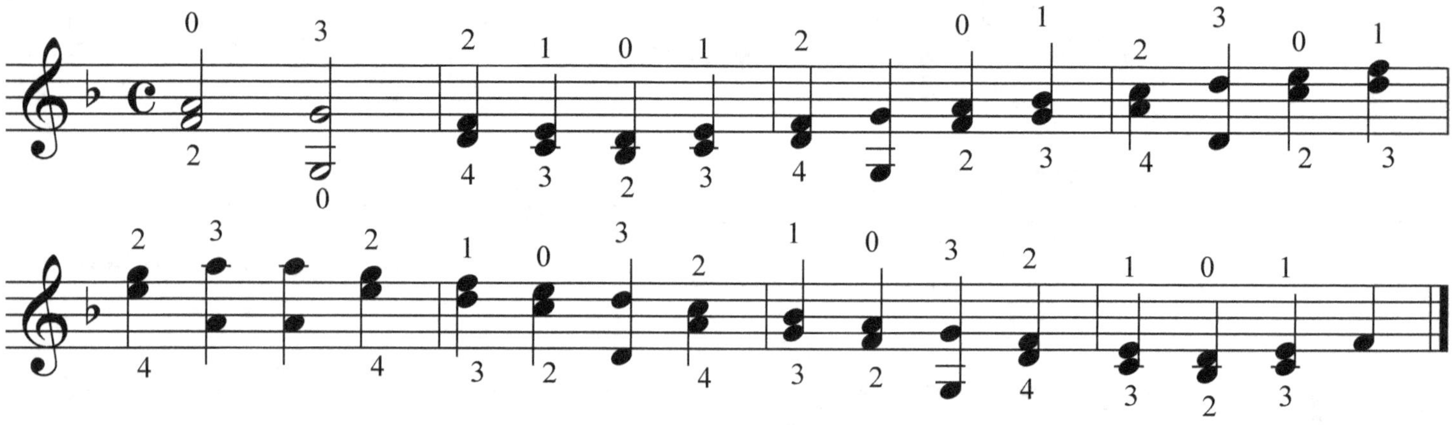

Thirds Etude No. 12

Double Stop Etudes for the Violin, Book One
41

F Major Exercise in Thirds and Octaves

Combination Etude No. 8

©2021 C. Harvey Publications All Rights Reserved.

F Major Exercise in Octaves

Octave Etude No. 2

Double Stop Etudes for the Violin, Book One

F Major Exercise in Fourths

Fourths Etude No. 5

©2021 C. Harvey Publications All Rights Reserved.

F Major Exercise in Fifths

Fifths Etude No. 4

Double Stop Etudes for the Violin, Book One
45

F Major: Changing Notes While Holding Notes

Slur Etude No. 4

©2021 C. Harvey Publications All Rights Reserved.

Part Five: B♭ Major

Learning Sixths in B♭ Major

Sixths Etude No. 11

Double Stop Etudes for the Violin, Book One

B♭ Exercise in Sixths

Sixths Etude No. 12

©2021 C. Harvey Publications All Rights Reserved.

Double Stop Etudes for the Violin, Book One

Learning Thirds in B♭ Major

Thirds Etude No. 13

Double Stop Etudes for the Violin, Book One

49

B♭ Exercise in Thirds

Thirds Etude No. 14

Double Stop Etudes for the Violin, Book One

B♭ Exercise in Sixths, Thirds, and Octaves

Combination Etude No. 9

Double Stop Etudes for the Violin, Book One

B♭ Exercise in Octaves

Octave Etude No. 3

B♭ Exercise in Fourths

Fourths Etude No. 6

Double Stop Etudes for the Violin, Book One

B♭ Exercise in Fifths

Fifths Etude No. 5

©2021 C. Harvey Publications All Rights Reserved.

Bb Major: Changing Notes While Holding Notes

Slur Etude No. 5

Part Six: Double Stop Scales in Other Keys

E♭ Major Scales

A♭ Major Scales

Double Stop Etudes for the Violin, Book One

D♭ Major Scales

F♯ Major Scales

Double Stop Etudes for the Violin, Book One
57

B Major Scales

E Major Scales

©2021 C. Harvey Publications All Rights Reserved.

A Major Scales

The Double Stop Series from C. Harvey Publications

Double Stop Beginnings for Violin, Book One (CHP247)

Double Stop Beginnings for Violin, Book Two (CHP248)

Double Stop Etudes for Violin, Book One (CHP406)

Double Stop Etudes for Violin, Book Two (with third position) - coming soon

Octaves for the Violin, Book One (CHP166)

Double Stop Shifting for Violin, Book One - coming soon

www.ingramcontent.com/pod-product-compliance
Lightning Source LLC
Chambersburg PA
CBHW081407070526
44583CB00020B/2712